Hurray for Three Kings' Day!

BY LORI MARIE CARLSON

ILLUSTRATED BY ED MARTINEZ

MORROW JUNIOR BOOKS

NEW YORK

For Sarah and Trevor Demaske,
and for Rosemary Brosnan,
whose spirit makes the month of January sweeter
—L.M.C.

To my children, Oliver and Gabriella
—E.M.

The full-color illustrations are oil paintings.
The text type is 15-point Phaistos Roman.
Book design by Christy Hale

Text copyright © 1999 by Lori Marie Carlson
Illustrations copyright © 1999 by Ed Martinez

Published by Morrow Junior Books
a division of William Morrow and Company, Inc.
1350 Avenue of the Americas, New York, NY 10019
www.williammorrow.com

Printed in Hong Kong by South China Printing Company (1988) Ltd.

10 9 8 7 6 5 4 3 2 1

Library of Congress Cataloging-in-Publication Data
Carlson, Lori M.
Hurray for Three Kings' Day!/by Lori Marie Carlson; illustrated by Ed Martinez.
p. cm.
Summary: A Hispanic family enjoys the traditional celebration of el Día de los Reyes,
or Epiphany, by reenacting the long walk of the three wise men bringing gifts to baby Jesus.
ISBN 0-688-16239-8 (trade)—ISBN 0-688-16240-1 (library)
I. Martinez, Ed, ill.   II. Title.   PZ7.C216633 Ri 1999   E—dc21   97-20937   CIP AC

When the beloved Puerto Rican librarian, Pura Belpré, started programs for Spanish-speaking children in New York in the 1940s and 1950s, she decided to emphasize Three Kings' Day, because she knew that all Latin Americans celebrated and respected this most special day of the year. She also wrote a short picture book about the Three Kings, in honor of the holiday. Today, Three Kings' Day is just as popular among people of Latino heritage, whether they live in Los Angeles, Rochester, New York City, Chicago, Albuquerque, or Miami.

Three Kings' Day actually begins on the evening before January sixth. The following morning, children find gifts that the kings have set out for them. Later that day, the festival culminates in the eating of a special cake and the naming of a king. The person whose cake slice hides a tiny ceramic or plastic figure is the chosen *rey,* or king.

The celebrations of Three Kings' Day vary from one Latino community to another. Venezuelan children, for example, put their shoes beside their beds to be filled with trinkets, and they sing carols. Puerto Rican children gather grass outside and then put it in a box underneath their beds in case the visiting camels are hungry. Mexican families eat *rosca de Reyes* cake. In my book, I have combined observances of several communities, so that the story appeals to the various groups that celebrate the holiday.

After Christmas Day, after New Year's, there is Epiphany,
or Three Kings' Day. In Spanish we say *el Día de los Reyes.*
My older brothers, Tito and Tomás, and I go walking in the
streets the night before, on January fifth, celebrating, singing,

laughing. But Tito and Tomás won't walk with me, because
they say that I'm a slowpoke.

"Hurry up, Anita," they yell, annoyed.

And I shout back, "I'm trying, *¿no lo ven?*"

We enter the procession in our little town, dressed in colors bursting like a sunset. We're the kings, three stargazers—Balthazar, Kaspar, and Melchior—also known as the Wise Men, or the Magi.

We carry gifts of make-believe gold, frankincense, and myrrh.

It's fun imagining that the herbs from Mama's kitchen—
saffron, lavender—are precious gifts. I especially like the smell
of mint. I want to make bouquets of all its rainy green.

On this holiday we visit friends and family to talk about and
remember the journey of the Wise Men, who followed a star
that they believed would take them to the birthplace of a child.

Arriving at the house of Mrs. Rosa, we pound on the door.
"Is this where we can find the child?" we ask, singing.

And Mrs. Rosa shakes her head, which is wrapped in a
silver turban. *"No, no, no, mis hijos."* So we go on.

But then I have to stop to exercise my toes. They tingle!
And they're cramped. I must have blisters.

The next house is Antonio's. He's a little hard of hearing.
When we knock loudly, his door opens.
We chant, "Is the tiny baby here?" and smile.
He adjusts his hearing aid. Then we repeat ourselves.
But Antonio says, *"Lo siento, mis amorcitos, pero no."*

Our feet are tired. And we're very sleepy. Me, especially.
I have to sit on the curb to rest from time to time.

Tito says, "Anita, you're a baby."
On we walk to Pepe's house. Pepe is a baker.

When Pepe opens his front door, we smell butter cookies in the oven, turning slowly golden, and the cinnamon and oranges of Christmas punch. "The child isn't here, but please, please, take these."

In our hands he places *los puerquitos*—piggy cookies.
  Tito and Tomás say they've had enough. Besides, they want
to help Papa with some grown-up chores. So we go home.

Inside, Mama hugs me. "Take your shoes off, *corazón,*" she says.
I sit down and pull them off. Then, according to the custom, I place
my shoes beside my bed, so the Three Kings will fill them with little
gifts. Next to the shoes I set down small boxes full of grass, flowers,

and hay and a bowl of water for the kings' camels to eat and drink.

My brothers laugh so hard, they start to hiccup. "No camels are coming to our house," they say. "Only babies believe that."

But I know they *will* come.

When I wake up, I see so many presents. Three puppets, one little
horse piñata, and boxes wrapped in bright red paper at the foot of my bed.

And I find a note about a special present somewhere else, maybe
in the living room. I run downstairs to see.

A lilac-painted dollhouse! Inside is a tiny wooden rocking chair.
Tomás runs outside to try his shiny silver bike. Tito starts setting
up his train track.

All day we play, until it's time for dinner. Then, *las estrellitas* wink at us. One large blazing star appears.

Later, in our house, we eat delicious feast-day foods—
albóndigas, papas, and *pavo*—that my parents, aunts, uncles,

and grandma have prepared for this Twelfth Night, twelve days after Christmas.

Afterward comes honey cake—*rosca de Reyes*—crispy,
sweet. And there is even more: *chocolate* and *piña, atoles* and
piñones. We eat until our stomachs ache.

As the plate of *postre* passes, each of us takes one big slice
of almond-decorated cake. We hold our breath to see who has
the prize—the traditional Reyes *muñequita,* the tiny doll that
Mama puts inside the cake before she bakes it.

"Whoever finds the doll receives a special treat," Papa says,
"just like the Reyes, who journeyed on and on and on because
they believed." They had faith.

My heart is pounding as I pick away the bits of lemon rind and pineapple. I scrape away the snow-white icing with my fingers.

As I nibble the sticky crumbs and oranges, pink cherries
from my fingertips, my tongue feels something hard—probably
a nut. But wait! It is the small clay doll.

I'm the king! Except, of course, that I'm a *reina,* I say proudly
to my brothers, not a *rey.*

GLOSSARY

albóndigas (al-BOHN-dee-gahs) meatballs

atoles (ah-TOH-lays) drinks made of cornmeal

chocolate (cho-co-LAH-tay) chocolate

corazón (ko-rah-ZOHN) heart

el Día de los Reyes (el DEE-ah day lohs RAY-yays) Three Kings' Day

las estrellitas (las ehs-tray-YEE-tahs) the little stars

los puerquitos (los puer-KEE-tohs) the little piggies

Lo siento, mis amorcitos, pero no. (Lo see-EN-toh, mees ah-mor-SEE-tohs,
  PEH-roh no) I'm sorry, my little sweethearts, but no.

mi hija (mee EE-hah) my daughter

muñequita (moon-yay-KEE-tah) little doll

¿no lo ven? (no lo behn) Don't you see?

No, no, no, mis hijos. (No, no, no, mees EE-hohs) No, no, no, my children.

papas (PAH-pahs) potatoes

pavo (PAH-boh) turkey

piña (PEEN-yah) pineapple

piñones (peen-YOHN-ays) pine nuts

postre (POHS-tray) dessert

reina (RAY-nah) queen

rosca de Reyes (ROS-ca day RAY-yays) Kings' cake